THE BABY
BILLIONAIRE
GUIDE TO INVESTING

*Building Wealth
at an
Early Age*

 THe Baby BilLioNaire™

IONNIE McNEILL

©2006 Ionnie McNeill

ISBN 978-0-9828031-3-4

Published by
Emerge Publishing Group, LLC
Riviera Beach, FL
877.363.7430
www.emergepublishers.com

Printed in the United States of America

ACKNOWLedgeMents

Mommy (Ann McNeill)
Daddy (Dan McNeill)
Sister (Danelle McNeill)
Malachi

International Mastermind Association
Better Investing (formerly National Association
of Investors Corporation)

The Howard University Legacy
The Washington, D.C. Community

Dedication

To all of my Family and Friends, in the
Known Universe

and

To the Youth of Today, Building
Wealth for Tomorrow

Contents

Concepts

"It requires a great deal of boldness and a great deal of caution to make a great fortune, and when you have it, it requires ten times as much skill to keep it."

~ Mark Twain

"Anyone can be great with money. With money, great-ness is not a talent but an obligation. The trick is to be great without money."

~ Albert Einstein

You Are Paying For What You Don't Know!

gnorance is expensive. Are you paying for what you don't know? Well rest assured,, we are all paying for what we don't know...in the form of "A Missed OPPORTUNITY." And one opportunity that we all have, regardless of money, education, or status, is TIME. You can probably agree that no matter who you are, what your social status is, or how much money you have, no one can ever get time back, once it has passed.

However, what you may not realize is that lost time is directly related to lost money. Every second that you live is a second that you cannot get back and the same is true with the opportunity to make money. Now I know that you are asking, "What is the relationship between time and money?" Think about it. Any time that you are not at work, you cannot get paid for it, right? Well, if you have never sent Your Money out to get a job and Work for You, then until this point, you have been missing the opportunity for Your Money to Work for You and bring home a couple of paychecks.

Yes, this is true and possible, and I'm sorry no one told you sooner. However, you *know* it now and I trust that you will *act* now. Therefore, don't allow many more opportunities to pass you by.

Not to delay you any longer, please know that this will be a very easy introduction to making your money work for you. In fact, if you recognize the word, "Investing" then you are already halfway there. You ready? Let's go!

"The greater the uncertainty, the more people are influenced by the market trends; and the greater the influence of trend following speculation, the more uncertain the situation becomes."

~ George Soros

A Conversation With The Baby Billionaire

I chose this journey before time and at this very moment I am sharing with you some of the principles that I learned in my childhood to help me be successful, by my own definition.

At the age of four years old, to be exact, I consciously began to mimic what I saw my Mother do, which was write goals for her life. Every Saturday morning my Mom and her girlfriends would mastermind together, setting goals in nine areas of their life and meeting regularly to hold each other accountable for the goals that they would set.

After watching them week after week and being the only child there, sitting silently listening to them, I naturally said to myself I want to do that, too. Therefore, without telling anyone, one Saturday I sat in on the meeting, as usual, but this time I had goals of my own written down, four to be exact. Well, being shy and hesitant, I didn't speak until the meeting was just about over and the ladies were packing up getting ready to leave. In a small voice I said, "I wanna read my goals." And one of my Mommy's friends said, "Oh honey, you can read your goals." So I read them, all four of them, and they included:

1. Get straight As

2. Play Basketball

3. Play Golf

4. Make a lot of Money

and that is exactly what happened. All throughout elementary, middle, high school, and even now in college, I have achieved those four goals. I'm on the Dean's List at Howard, I was on a 3-time State Championship Basketball Team in High School, I have continued to play golf throughout school, and now I'm on the road to making a lot of money, through investing.

With time my goals have grown and expanded, along with my successes and achievements, but it was at a young age that my foundation was laid because I realized the importance of writing my goals, creating an action plan to reach my goals, and being steadfast in achieving my goals. When you hear older people say, "I wish I knew then what I know now," doesn't it make sense to capitalize on their wisdom and not make the same mistake?

I felt this was important to share with you, so that you could see the beginning steps of success. Therefore, Dream BIG! Write what you want. Then start immediately working to make it a reality. What are you waiting on? A pen and a pad? Well, I've provided the pad and with you bringing the writing utensil, use the next two pages to write what you envision your life to be.

My Life's Goals

_____

_____

_____

_____

_____

_____

_____

_____

_____

_____

_____

_____

_____

_____

_____

_____

_____

_____

_____

_____

_____

_____

_____

_____

My Life's Goals

_____

_____

_____

_____

_____

_____

_____

_____

_____

_____

_____

_____

_____

_____

_____

_____

_____

_____

_____

_____

_____

"Riches do not respond to wishes. They respond only to definite plans, backed by definite desires, through constant PERSISTENCE."

~ Napoleon Hill

"Many of the things you can count, don't count. Many of the things you can't count, really count."

~ Ralph Waldo Emerson

WHere AM I GoiNg?

From my own life experience, you can see, setting goals in life is essential in charting your course and helping you know where you want to go. In fact, we do it every day, even if we don't realize it. For example, if you made a decision to get food from McDonald's, then that would be the goal. The next step you would take is to decide the best way to get there. Is it by walking or driving? Think about it. Whenever you get in a car, don't you know where the end destination is? Whether it is your school or grandmother's house, you know beforehand where you are going. And even if you don't know how to get there, you can find the directions using the internet or the navigation system in your car. Well, life is the same way. Once you have an idea of where you want to go, map out a route that can help you get there.

Now that you are a PRO at setting small goals in life, I know that you will be just as great at setting big goals. In fact, I'm already sure that you have started. Let's see… Have you thought about what type of career you want to have when you grow up? Well, what about a house, a car, or even money? Well, if you said yes to any of these questions, then you have already started creating your goals. Now, all we have to do is make them concrete, so that you can actively make them a reality.

With you already being smart, you have to also make sure that your goals are SMART as well, which stands for: **S**pecific

Measurable

Attainable

Realistic

Timely

I know this will be easy for you to remember. These are the characteristics of great goals. In a book titled, *"Think and Grow Rich,"* the author Napoleon Hill says that, "It is not merely enough to say 'I want a lot of money', you must be specific… $50, $100, $100,000, or any definite amount." The reason for this is so that you can actually measure whether or not you have reached your goal. The phrase "A Lot of Money" can represent different amounts for different people; so it's imperative to be *specific*.

Your goals also have to be *measurable* so that it is clear to you when you have reached them. Therefore, it is not sufficient to just say, "I want to be happy". Describe what happy is to you. What does it mean to be happy (in your own definition)? Meanwhile, ask yourself, "Why aren't I happy now?" Be sure not to attach your happiness to material things because if you are only happy when you have these things, what will happen when these things go away? Happiness should come from within and should not be determinant on outside factors, meaning you can be happy even before you get the shoes, clothes, car, money, status, or relationship that you want and are waiting for.

Make sure that your goals are *attainabl*e and *realistic*. It would be unrealistic to say that you want $1 million by tomorrow and you don't even have $100 yet. Give yourself enough time to reach your

BIG goals after you have set them. Lastly, ensure your goals are *timely*. Set a specific point in time, an exact date, by when you would like to reach your goal. This allows you to effectively plan the necessary steps to make your dream a reality, from now until then. For example, if I said, "I want to graduate from college," do you think that is a "SMART" goal? Well, how about this, "I plan to graduate from Howard University with a Bachelor Degree in Business Administration, while maintaining a 3.8 GPA in May 2010"?

As you can see the more specific and descriptive you make your goal, the more you can visualize it, measure it, and make it a reality. So again, dare to Dream BIG and think about what you want to be, do, and have in life. Then make it as detailed as possible and start immediately towards making it a reality. And if you don't know where to start, just continue to think about your goals and in time, opportunities will soon be revealed to you.

Now that you know, or at least have an idea, where you are going, we can begin to plan your map to get there. As you already know, MONEY is the medium of exchange that most people use in order to get the things they want out of life. Therefore, let's explore the possibilities of using money to help you reach your goals.

HoW CaN I Get THere?

With your goals already set, let's discuss how to use time to your advantage. By understanding the *Time Value of Money*, you can easily begin putting your money to work for you.

As you may already know, a dollar today is worth more than a dollar tomorrow or even a year from now. Why? Because of inflation. Inflation can be seen in the rise in food and gas prices from year to year. As time progresses, it takes more money to buy the things we need on a regular basis. For example, when I was in elementary school, a 12oz. can of soda cost $.25. In middle school, the same can rose to $.50. In high school it rose again to $.75. Now that I'm in college, it is close to $1. As you can see, even though the amount of soda didn't change, its price definitely increased over time.

In order for us to stay ahead of the devaluation of money, we must make our money grow. "How do we make it grow?" you ask. Through interest. By putting your money to work, you can earn interest, which is a percentage paid to you for letting someone else use it. That's where we come to the concepts of Saving and Investing.

SAVING

When most people hear the word saving, they think of a savings account (at a credit union or bank) or a coin jar/piggy bank at home. By having your money in a savings account you can earn interest that you would not earn otherwise if it was in your piggy bank or your pocket.

Most savings accounts pay you interest for keeping your money with them. How are they able to do this? Well, when you think about how a bank works, it uses other people's money to make money. To explain further, it takes the money from your savings and checking account and uses it as loans to other people and businesses.

Think about this, what if I borrowed $100 from you and told you that I would return it next week, plus another dollar. And once you gave me the $100, I lent it to my friend and charged him $10 to use it for a week. By the following week, my friend would have given me $110 and I would give you $101. So, in the end, I would have made $9. Well, this is the same concept for understanding how banks work. They borrow your money, by using your deposits in the bank account, and pay you a low interest rate, while lending the same money out to others but charging them a higher interest rate, and keeping the difference for themselves.

INVESTING

So now that you understand saving, investing is just as simple. In fact, the concept is the same except the middle man, me in the last example, is not needed therefore you are able to receive more interest. But before getting too deep into investing let's talk more about interest.

Simple Interest

If someone pays you simple interest, they are only paying you a set percentage on your initial investment, or beginning value. For example, if you were to receive 10% on your $100, then you would earn $10 in the 1st year, $10 in the 2nd year, 3rd year, and so on. See Below

Year 1:	10% of $100	= 10 + 100	= $110.00
Year 2:	10% of $100	= 10 + 110	= $120.00
Year 3:	10% of $100	= 10 + 120	= $130.00
Year 4:	10% of $100	= 10 + 130	= $140.00
Year 5:	10% of $100	= 10 + 140	= $150.00

Compound Interest

On the other hand, compound interest is a little more attractive. It is the only one that allows you to earn interest on your original investment and on the interest you made before. So, using the same $100 and 10% interest rate, your returns will look more like this:

Year 1: 10% of $100   = 10 + 100   = $110.00

Year 2: 10% of $110   = 11 + 110   = $121.00

Year 3: 10% of $121   = 12.1 + 121   = $133.10

Year 4: 10% of $133.10 = 13.31 + 133.10 = $146.41

Year 5: 10% of $146.41 = 14.64 + 146.41 = $161.05

Therefore, the earlier you start investing, the more time your money has to work for you, at an exponential rate because of compound interest.

An *Interesting* Illustration

Simple Growth:

Compounded Growth:

THE TIME VALUE OF MONEY—Invest Now Rather Than Later

Billy Investing at Age 15 (10% Return)			Susan Investing at Age 19 (10% Return)			Kim Investing at Age 27 (10% Return)		
Age	Invest $3K/yr	Value	Age	Invest $3K/yr	Value	Age	Invest $3K/yr	Value
15	$3K	$3,300.00	15			15		
16	$3K	$6,930.00	16			16		
17	$3K	$10,923.00	17			17		
18	$3K	$15,315.30	18			18		
19	$3K	$20,146.83	19	$3K	$3,300.00	19		
20		$22,161.51	20	$3K	$6,930.00	20		
21		$24,377.66	21	$3K	$10,923.00	21		
22		$26,815.43	22	$3K	$15,315.30	22		
23		$29,496.97	23	$3K	$20,146.83	23		
24		$32,446.67	24	$3K	$25,461.51	24		
25		$35,691.34	25	$3K	$31,307.66	25		
26		$39,260.47	26	$3K	$37,738.43	26		
27		$43,186.52	27		$41,512.27	27	$3K	$3,300.00
28		$47,505.17	28		$45,663.50	28	$3K	$6,930.00
29		$52,255.69	29		$50,229.85	29	$3K	$10,923.00
30		$57,482.26	30		$55,252.84	30	$3K	$15,315.30
31		$63,229.38	31		$60,778.12	31	$3K	$20,146.83
32		$69,552.32	32		$66,885.93	32	$3K	$25,461.51
33		$76,507.55	33		$73,541.53	33	$3K	$31,307.66
34		$84,158.31	34		$80,895.68	34	$3K	$37,738.43
35		$92,574.14	35		$88,985.25	35	$3K	$44,812.27
36		$101,831.55	36		$97,883.77	36	$3K	$52,593.50
37		$112,014.71	37		$107,672.15	37	$3K	$61,152.85
38		$123,216.18	38		$118,439.36	38	$3K	$70,568.14
39		$135,537.80	39		$130,283.30	39	$3K	$80,924.95
40		$149,091.58	40		$143,311.63	40	$3K	$92,317.45
41		$164,000.74	41		$157,642.79	41	$3K	$104,849.19
42		$180,400.81	42		$173,407.07	42	$3K	$118,634.11
43		$198,440.89	43		$190,747.78	43	$3K	$133,797.52
44		$218,284.98	44		$209,822.55	44	$3K	$150,477.27
45		$240,113.48	45		$230,804.81	45	$3K	$168,825.00
46		$264,124.82	46		$253,885.29	46	$3K	$189,007.50
47		$290,537.31	47		$279.273.82	47	$3K	$211,208.25
48		$319,591.04	48		$307,201.20	48	$3K	$235,629.07
49		$351,550.14	49		$337,921.32	49	$3K	$262,491.98
50		$386,705.16	50		$371,713.45	50	$3K	$292,041.18
51		$425,375.67	51		$408,884.80	51	$3K	$324,545.30
52		$467,913.24	52		$449,773.28	52	$3K	$360,299.83
53		$514,704.56	53		$494,750.61	53	$3K	$399,629.81
54		$566,175.02	54		$544,225.67	54	$3K	$442,892.79
55		$622,792.52	55		$598,648.24	55	$3K	$490,482.07
56		$685,071.77	56		$658.513.06	56	$3K	$542,830.27
57		$753,578.95	57		$724,364.36	57	$3K	$600,413.30
58		$828,936.84	58		$796,800.80	58	$3K	$663,754.63
59		$911,830.53	59		$876,480.88	59	$3K	$733,430.10
60		$1,003,013.58	60		$964,128.97	60	$3K	$810,073.11
61		$1,103,314.94	61		$1,060,541.87	61	$3K	$894,380.42
62		$1,213,646.43	62		$1,166,596.05	62	$3K	$987,118.46
63		$1,335,011.08	63		$1,283,255.66	63	$3K	$1,089,130.30
64		$1,468,512.18	64		$1,411,581.22	64	$3K	$1,201,343.33
65		**$1,615,363.40**	**65**		**$1,552,739.35**	**65**		**$1,324,777.67**

Total Invested = $15,000 Billy's Earnings Beyond Investment = $1,600,363.40	Total Invested = $24,000 Susan's Earnings Beyond Investment = $1,528,739.35	Total Invested = $117,000 Kim's Earnings Beyond Investment = $1,207,777.67

Returns on all invest products will fluctuate. Investment return and principal value will fluctuate and your investment value may be more or less than the original amount.

Billy invested $102,000 less than Kim and has $290,585.73 more!

START INVESTING EARLY!

HoW Do I See MoNey?

Years ago when I first laid my eyes on the "Time Value of Money Chart" I was motivated to make my money grow. Instantly, my entire attitude about money changed and I was determined to start investing early, rather than late.

How do you see money? Is it a means to an end or the end itself? By watching our parents pay for things with money and listening to friends make plans on what they were going to purchase, we automatically learned how to spend money.

But there is so much more to money than its capacity to be spent. In this capitalistic society, it is your power. Yes, Your POWER! Every time you buy something to eat from McDonald's, you are giving McDonald's your **power** in exchange for its products.

Therefore, be more conscious of how you use your power and who you give your power to. Yes, you need to buy food, clothes, and other things that you may want, but also consider what it is that you are buying, whom you are buying it from, and if it is beneficial to you.

Money has the capacity to grow, in addition to being spent, as we have seen in earlier chart. So be mindful of your view on money and don't limit it to just spending. You wouldn't want to miss out on the opportunity of time because you always gave in to instant gratification.

The best strategy is to do both, spend money on items you need, then invest in the companies you just bought from. There, you can have your cake and eat it, too. Soon we'll discuss how to actually start investing.

"Rich people see every dollar as a "seed" that can be planted to earn a hundred more dollars, which can then be replant- ed to earn a thousand more dollars."

~T. Harv Eker.

WHO AM I EMPOWERING ALONG THE WAY?

Now that you know that your money is your power, think about how others are using your power to further their goals and objectives. Ask yourself, are their values aligned with mine and do I agree with their practices? When you consider spending your money with an institution or company, consider its impact on you and your community. Who are the owners?

Who do they hire to be employees? Do they reinvest money in your community?

When you become an investor, you are also a shareholder, which is defined as a part owner of a company. Being a shareholder gives you power and influence because you can participate in the management and ownership decisions in the company. For example, every year each public company has an annual meeting, which all of the owners are invited to attend. It is at this meeting that the company gives its performance report to its shareholders and the shareholders, who in turn vote on important topics such as who will be on the Board of Directors, how products should be produced, and various policies that should govern the corporation.

So, why not let your voice be heard? You have the opportunity to learn how business is done and share your ideas on where the company should go in the future. I encourage you to become active in corporate decisions, while you make money. It will make your investing journey much more exciting.

Remember, your money is your power, so it can be used in ways other than just being exchanged for products and services. It is your Voice and your Vote. Therefore, use your voice and vote to demand support from the institutions that you already empower as a consumer by spending your money there. Companies that you support and patronize should also support you and your community, whether it is through educational scholarships, organizational sponsorships, or even mentoring programs to help you explore the different career options that are available to you in the future.

"Money will buy a bed but not sleep; books but not brains; food but not appetite; finery but not beauty; a house but not a home; medicine but not health; luxuries but not culture; amusements but not happiness; religion but not salvation; a passport to everywhere but heaven."

~unknown

HoW CaN I Start INvestiNg?

N ow you're on the road to buying your first stock! This is where we get to work. Since you learn best by doing, grab a computer, pull up the Internet, and we'll walk through the steps of getting started.

First, go to the website of your favorite company, whether you shop there often or use their products on a regular basis, for example, Nike, Apple, Procter

& Gamble, Wal-Mart, The Home Depot, and others. Once you are there, click on Investor Relations, also called Stock Information, which should be located on the top, bottom, or left-hand side of the company's home page.

Next, on the left side of the new page, there should be a section entitled Direct Stock Purchase Plan or Dividend Reinvestment Plan (DRIP). If so, click on it. This will bring you to either a pdf (Adobe) file that you can print, or a page that says they use Computershare or another type of low-cost investment service provider for its Direct Stock Purchase Plan program.

From here, it is all smooth sailing. Just fill-out the form with the information requested:

1. Your First and Last Name:

_____

- If you are under 18, include the name of one of your parents as the Guardian/ Custodian

2.. Your Social Security Number:_____

3. Mailing Address:_____

4. Your Signature:_____

- If you are under 18, have the Guardian Custodian sign it

5. Date:_____

Just five easy items can get you on your way to taking advantage of the greatest opportunity you have, TIME. And if you are over 18 and buying stock for someone who is under 18, either related or unrelated, then you would put your name as the guardian and register the stock under the child's name and social security number.

If you were redirected to Computershare or any other third-party company to buy the stock directly from the company, not to worry, it is just as easy. When you get to their site, the steps should be the same, if not similar.

Once your application form is completed and your check is made out, or bank information included if you decided to join their Automatic Investment plan, then mail the information to the mailing address provided and within a few weeks you should receive your stock statement (which looks like a bank statement). Before I forget, when filling out your application form, be sure to check the option box that you want the "Full Dividend Reinvestment". This is very important because it allows your investment to grow at a compounded rate, which is like the chart we saw on page 26 (Chapter 4).

Now that you see how easy this process is, use the next page to list a few of your favorite companies that you are already familiar with or are interested in. Then research their Direct Stock Purchase Plans or DRIPs.

Prospective Investments

_____

_____

_____

_____

_____

_____

_____

_____

_____

_____

_____

_____

_____

_____

_____

_____

_____

_____

_____

_____

_____

_____

_____

_____

Where Can I Go to Continue Learning?

Finally, let's talk about continuing education. Just like anything we do or are involved in, it must be reinforced outside of the classroom. It is only the things that we do repeatedly that we become good at. Therefore, reading this book was only the beginning of your investing journey. Supplement this with other financial books to ensure you increase your personal power called finances.

The easiest way to continue to learn this information is to be around people who are willing to teach you and learn with you. One great way to do this is through an "investment club". Whether you start one or join one, you should surround yourself with similar minded people, who are seeking to educate themselves on investing and make money in the process.

Better Investing is a premiere organization to join and participate in because of its dedication to providing a program of sound investment information, education, and support, creating successful lifetime investors (and some millionaires in the process). Since it is a national organization, they have local chapters in almost every state and can be located online at www.betterinvesting.org. In fact, it was by attending Better Investing's classes and conferences that I learned how to start investing, and that was when I was seven years old. So, needless to say, the concepts, methodology, and information it teaches is easy to understand and effortless to implement. Therefore, become a member and begin to reap the benefits of investing. Why Wait?

CONGRATULATIONS on your start! This is only the beginning. Soon you will be able to truly understand any financial material you read. Be sure to reinforce the learning process through reading more books like this, discussing what you learned with others, and attending classes offered by Better Investing.

Also, check out some of the suggested books listed below, they will be sure to get you on your way.

- *In Search of the Green* by Patricia E. Edwards

- *The Automatic Millionaire* by David Bach

- *The Motley Fool Investment Guide for Teens* by David and Tom Gardner

- *The Teen's Guide to Personal Finance* by Joshua Holmberg and David Bruzzese

- *You've Earned It, Don't Lose It* by Suze Orman

- *Rich Dad, Poor Dad* by Robert Kiyosaki

- *Think and Grow Rich* by Napoleon Hill

5 THiNgS BaBy BiLLiONaireS SHoULd KNoW aNd Do

1. Recognize that TIME is the most important asset you have

2. Start Investing NOW

3. Become OWNERS of the companies you buy from

4. Knowledge is only potential Power, but Applied Knowledge is POWERFUL

5. Have FUN and make your money work for you

"If you do not see great riches in your imagination, you will never see them in your bank balance."

~ Napoleon Hill

"He that is of the opinion money will do everything may well be suspected of doing everything for money."

~Benjamin Franklin

FAMOUS Quotes FroM Billionaires

"Rule No.1: Never lose money. Rule No.2: Never forget rule No.1."

Warren Buffett

CEO of Berkshire Hathaway

"When you live for others' opinions, you are dead."

Carlos Slim Helu

CEO of Telmex, América Móvil, Grupo Carso

"If you can count your money, you don't have a billion dollars."

J. Paul Getty

Founder of Getty Oil Company

"Only those who are asleep make no mistakes."

Ingvar Kamprad

Founder of IKEA

"We're going where no one has gone before. There's no model to follow, nothing to copy. That is what makes this so exciting."

Richard Branson
Chairman of Virgin Group

"You can't just ask customers what they want and then try to give that to them. By the time you get it built, they'll want something new."

Steve Jobs
Co-founder of Apple

"You become what you believe. You are where you are today in your life based on everything you have believed."

Oprah Winfrey

CEO of Oprah Winfrey Network

"We're all working together; that's the secret."

Sam Walton

Founder of Walmart

"The secret of business is to know something that nobody else knows."

Aristotle Onassis

Greek Shipping Magnate

"As I grow older, I pay less attention to what men say. I just watch what they do."

Andrew Carnegie

Founder of Carnegie Steel Company

I never attempt to make money on the stock market. "I buy on the assumption that they could close the market the next day and not reopen it for five years."

Warren Buffett

Investor/Stock Market Guru

Everyone experiences tough times, it is a measure of your determination and dedication how you deal with them and how you can come through them.

Lakshmi Mittal

Owner of the world's largest steel company ArcelorMittal

"I believe that if a businessman knows how to efficiently manage his business, he should be able to manage a foundation efficiently. It's not a question of giving money away, it's a question of going somewhere and doing something and making sure the basic costs are paid...I'm channeling resources to try to solve problems as quickly as possible."

Carlos Slim Helu

Communications Businessman and Invest

"The typical human life seems to be quite unplanned, undirected, unlived, and unsavored. Only those who consciously think about the adventure of living as a matter of making choices among options, which they have found for themselves, ever establish real self-control and live their lives fully."

Karl Albrecht

Co-Founder of Supermarket Giant Aldi

"I think that our fundamental belief is that for us growth is a way of life and we have to grow at all times".

Mukesh Amban

Chairman & Managing Director of
Reliance Industries

"Getting the job done has been the basis for the success my company has achieved."

Michael Bloomberg

Founder of Bloomberg Financial Media Company
and New York Mayor

"They're real life demonstrations of the biblical adage 'If you give a man a fish, he'll eat for a day. If you teach the man to fish, he'll eat for a lifetime.'"

David Koch

Executive Vice President, Koch Industries

"It's through curiosity and looking at opportunities in new ways that we've always mapped our path at Dell. There's always an opportunity to make a difference."

Michael Dell

Founder and Chairman of Dell Computers

Everyone experiences tough times, it is a measure of your determination and dedication how you deal with them and how you can come through them.

Lakshmi Mittal

Owner of the world's largest steel company ArcelorMittal

"The role of business is to produce goods and services that make people's lives better. And if you have to get a subsidy–if you have to force other people to support your profit–you're not doing that. You're not making them better off; you're making them worse off."

Charles Koch

Head of Koch Industries

About the Author

Ionnie McNeill is a recent graduate of Howard University in Washington, DC, and currently a professional speaker on youth investing. At age 7, Ionnie began her investment education and by age 10 already had a portfolio invested in stocks and bonds. Since then she has traveled across the nation, including New York, Philadelphia, Chicago, Atlanta and Milwaukee, WI speaking to youth (and adults) about the importance and benefits of investing at an early age. As a result of her endeavors, Ionnie has been featured in magazines such as *Black Enterprise, Seventeen, Better Investing,* and newspapers including, *The Miami Herald* and the *Chicago Defender*. Recently, she was also a key panelist at the ESSENCE Young

Women's Leadership Conference in November 2008 and a Finalist Winner in the Ford/HBCU Business Plan Competition featured on TVOne. Even in high school, Ionnie was making her mark by being awarded 1st place in the Guardian's Girls Going Places Entrepreneurship Awards Program, for the work The Baby Billionaire has done.

In June 2010, The Baby Billionaire has successfully hosted its 3rd National Youth Investing Conference in partnership with Better Investing, the leader in investment education. And recently, she was featured in January 2011 issue of *ESSENCE* Magazine for her accomplishments in building wealth at an early age. Now, Ionnie travels the world creating memorable and transformational financial learning experiences for her clients and the next generation.

www.thebabybillionaire.com

Ionniemcneill@yahoo.com

www.ingramcontent.com/pod-product-compliance
Lightning Source LLC
Chambersburg PA
CBHW060646210326
41520CB00010B/1756